praise for FIG

The poetic forms in this chapbook are crafted with a perfectly sharpened knife. Dear Reader, sit with these poems as if dining at an old wood table among friends and savor each slow moment. *Fig* is a most "delicious listening."
— Vivian Faith Prescott, poet and author of *My Father's Smokehouse: Stories and Recipes from Fishcamp*

Emily Wall is a master of language and insight. Sensuous and spare, in the voice and life of Alice Waters, Wall has created poetic recipes of love and attention to all that matters. Each word—fresh and exactly in its place. These poems will ". . show you/ the way to live in the warm/ center of your life." Go hungry. Be satiated!
— Wendy Erd, author of *It's a Crooked Road but Not Far to the House of Flowers*

After devouring *Flame* and *Fist*, I eagerly awaited *Fig*, the third in this trilogy about passionate, powerful, trailblazing women. ... Emily Wall is a master of persona poems, revealing the essence of these women in a way that opens the doors wide for us all to live our own best life. Brava!
— Marybeth Holleman, author of *Tender Gravity* and *The Heart of the Sound*

Wall's poetry is evocative and sensual-- inspiring the reader to consider, deeply, the magic of food, cooking, and the natural world we are part of.
— Renée Jakaitis Trafton, Chef and Owner, Beak Restaurant and James Beard Best Chefs Semi-Finalist 2023

fig

emily wall

MINERVA RISING PRESS
Boca Raton

Cover art by Tijana Drndarski
Book design by Brooke Schultz

ISBN 978-1-950811-19-9

Printed and bound in USA
First Printing March 2022

Published by Minerva Rising Press
17717 Circle Pond Ct
Boca Raton, FL 33496

For my three delicious girls,
and for my husband Corey.

For Alice Waters, with thanks
for her encouragement to write
these poems.

With gratitude to everyone who
supports the Douglas Food
Pantry.

Fig is part of a chapbook trilogy written in the wake of the 2016 election. Encapsulating the voices of three powerful women: Mary, mother of Jesus; Georgia O'Keeffe, artist and feminist pioneer; and Alice Waters, chef and food activist. Through persona poems, each book seeks to speak to and lift up women, who are living with trauma and fear, in this current political climate.

Flame and Fist, the other two books in the trilogy, are also available from Minerva Rising Press.

Don't ever lose that sense of independence.
Or doubt it. It's your greatest strength.
Even if the way that you're seeing things feels like
the loneliness place in the world. Trust it.
It's the greatest thing any one of us can do, actually.
Is to trust our instincts.

— Alice Waters, Note to Self

contents

About these poems

These are persona and poetic form poems.

Persona: I've borrowed the "mask" of Alice to tell her story, and of course my own story. This is the magic of persona poems to me: they allow us to enter our own stories in a safe way, and they encourage us to blend our stories and songs. In studying Alice's life, I've found the story of a fiercely independent woman, who uses her wisdom and skills to create family, and who sees feeding that family as important political work. Each meal she creates is a powerful statement reminding us who we truly are and how food informs our identities and belief systems. She reminds us that choosing one beautiful piece of fruit is an act of revolution. I've loved the years I've spent learning about Alice and her work and I hope you too will enjoy your time living in these poems.

Form: In the spirit of recipes and the deep perfection of Chez Panisse food, each poem is crafted in a poetic form.

Amuse Bouche: a pantoum
How a Girl Learns to Shout: an Italian sonnet
How to Comfort Your Tongue: an extended haiku

All of the Sorbet poets: hay(na)kus

How to be Hungry: rhyming couplets
How to Hold Hot Tea: an extended tanka
How to Scavenge What You Need: a haibun

AMUSE BOUCHE

A bowl of warm milk made from wild grass.
From Frog Hollow Farm: one split fig.
Garlic. Artichoke. One seductive olive.
This is how much you should love your body.

From Frog Hollow Farm: one sliced-wide fig.
You sit in the shade of an acacia, massage your palms—
yes, this is how much you should love your body.
Make yourself a tender omelet: eggs, butter, chervil.

You sit in the shade of an acacia, massage your palms:
you smell garlic, artichoke. Seductive olives.
Now, make tenderness: with eggs, butter, chervil,
with a bowl of warm milk, with these wild grasses.

fig | 1

HOW A GIRL
LEARNS TO SHOUT

Berkeley is burning. I sit on my bed, try to read,
but the chanting rises. In the corner rests a sign
protesting the arrests. My professor says in his time
girls didn't shout at men. I look to the men leading
the charge, watch them link arms, watch them leave
in handcuffs. Could I? I imagine my hands tied
and take a step back. I answer phones, drive
a candidate to his rallies. *Is this all a woman can be?*

I walk through the farmer's market, dream up dishes,
let my fingers touch asparagus, tomatoes, snap peas.
We are not the bombs we drop, the women we silence.
We are not supermarkets full of frozen, packaged fish.
I buy a huge table, then open my door: *come, eat.*
A handful of chives in my pan, breaks my silence.

HOW TO FIND YOUR NAME

— in London

The color palate
of my plate: fierce yellow, bright
red: fire my tongue.

cardamom

Yogurt raita
paired with tandoori chicken—
my whole throat opens.

cumin

Spices sizzling
on the stove. I close my eyes—
delicious listening.

coriander

fig | 3

Steaming basmati
rice. Tiny little courses
both sour and sweet.

cassia

The smell of fire
burning in the clay tandoor.
I can breathe again.

clove

My usual please.
A prawn and spinach curry—
here, this is my name.

SORBET

Palm
perfectly shaped
to hold knife.

fig | 5

HOW TO BE HUNGRY

— in Paris

Back home is burning.
Here, my tongue learns

> *café, fromagerie,*
> *boulangerie, pâtisserie.*

> Fingers push buttons
> through small mouths, hungry hungry

> wild strawberries, sugar shaker
> a deep spoon of *crème fraîche.*

I'll sleep with him if I want to, this Parisian man.
I'll slip him a peeled egg, still warm from the pan

> then skip class. Back home: nice girls,
> quiet girls, zipped up, stand-up straight girls.

> But here: I push open the door
> brass knob warm, in cool mist morning

> *s'il vous plait, un croissant*
> *s'il vous plait, un pain au chocolat.*

Skin infused with cream, with sweet *framboise*—
say it, tongue and teeth: *c'est chez moi.*

        This is how much
                my body should be loved.

fig | 7

HOW TO HOLD
HOT TEA
— *Italy, Greece, Turkey*

I didn't know this
but a woman can't travel
      by herself. In a
café the waiter walks right
by. Thinks I'm a prostitute.

              One night I meet a
          German man. We can't speak to
                each other. But oh
          the gesture of his hand when
              he calls me into his bed.

                    In Greece we meet up
              with two French men who have hash.
                  We drive cars on dunes
                of wild sand, free falling
                  into the salty rich sea.

In small Turkish towns
two women driving their car
        can't enter safely.
We pretend our drug dealers
are husbands. They drive, we drink.

Strangers invite us
to a wedding. The men and
women part. All night
we women henna our hands
and dance to the tambourine.

Then one night, we girls
raise our tent in a small field.
We don't know it's owned
by shepherds. In the morning
we find a bowl of warm milk.

fig | 9

HOW TO SCAVENGE
WHAT YOU NEED

— with Martine

At the flea market, we slip cloth between our fingers. Gathered, shirred,
softly draping. My French friend knows how to tie curtains—just so. How
to pick flawless lamps. Copper, mismatched. We run our palms across
patchwork quilts, warm fabrics, that make us feel at home. Even in a place
we've never been—a small village in Tuscany, a farmhouse in Georgia—
home. We pick plates, always white, never matching. Pullman car candle-
sticks. Pink Victorian glasses. Forks: below their patina, a soft shine. Forks
I can imagine on the tables I'll buy and arrange in the house on Shattuck
Avenue. Oak tables, white plates, silver forks. You could sit at a table with
your friend, and maybe a filmmaker she wants you to meet. Copper lights,
buttery bright. You'll talk about songs, misogyny, poems, pesticides, racism,
the man without a home named Sam. You each lift a bite of fruit tarte.
Taste the same bright fruit, the same crunch of sugar, each bite resting on a
fork that has its own voice.

I sift for treasure.
My hands choose what I need to
build a family.

SORBET

Tongue
always ready
to lift me.

fig | **11**

HOW TO EAT
THE WILD

Go. Find fennel, berries, morels from the tracks,
a small gathering of wild bamboo.
Tonight we'll serve them the taste of wild grass.

A neighbor calls: she has lemons. We fill her glass
with pure water: one crush, and she will tell you
to go find fennel, berries, morels from the tracks.

Look at her. After drinking this lemon she understands:
no food wrapped in plastic, under lights, sickly blue.
Tonight we served her the taste of wild grass.

A man comes in, eyes creased, hands cracked,
holding a fresh duck: can this be used?
Go. Find fennel, berries, morels from the tracks,

chives, nasturtiums, asparagus. Remember back—
our ancestors didn't ask if this was the right thing to do.
Tonight, we'll serve him the taste of wild grass.

On a white plate, acacia blossoms, just gathered.
This is how to eat the world. Want to join us too?
Go. Find fennel, berries, morels from the tracks.
Tonight, we'll serve you the taste of wild grass.

HOW TO CHANGE
A THOUSAND MINDS

Where do we begin? With butter.
We begin with the cow, the grass, the light
falling on a farm in Petaluma. The way it gilds
the grasses that will be eaten. The way it warms
the rich, black soil. Look at that lemony
field, at that cow, the way she moves, the crush

of clover underfoot. What we begin with, is a crush
on food. I think of Tom, and the way he butters
an omelet he's made for me, under one lemony
lamp: omelet, chervil, butter, tongue. Lightly
sweet: teeth. We all want this. A pool of warmth
at the end of every day, after the riot of this gilded

city. And from the butter, comes this: gilt-edged
mirrors that show the chef behind you, crushing
cumin and coriander for the lamb. The wood fire warms
her hands, as she works. Next to her, a cook blots butter
lettuce, one leaf at a time. If you want to gather light
from a farm and plate it, you change your breath: one lemon

fig | 13

slice on a white plate. Breathe lemon, only lemon.
When all you have is one piece of fruit, it becomes gilded
as a picture, hanging in the Louvre. As do you, sitting in light,
hands picking up this slice. Feel its silky texture. Now crush
it in your Pellegrino. Inhale. Your mind leaps to buttery
cheese you had once, in Provence, small café, on a warm

autumn day. Suddenly a laugh at the next table warms
you. You look at this man, his laugh, sweet as lemonade
on a hot day. Something in your knees feels buttery,
meaty. You are both eating mesclun, leaves lightly gilded
with oil, and this connects you. Of course you have a crush
on him. What would he be like to kiss? His hand light

on your back, as you head home, walking a night lightly
scented with oranges. You've finally acted: plated warm
food in a soup kitchen, fought the patriarchy. You are crushing
the food industrial complex. No more pesticides on our lemons.
Why did we think this was impossible? We peel that layer of gild
off the American lily. We are field, grasses, cows. Butter.

Now, I bring you a lemon soufflé. Go ahead. Gild your tongue
with its buttery center. When you leave, carry this crush with you.
This light. The warmth of this beginning.

HOW TO LIGHT
EACH OTHER

I move between tables, light in my hands, framed.
At each, I lift the copper lantern, light the wick,
see in dozens of mirrors: that leap of flame.

You stand in the door. A silver candlestick
gleams. I cross the room, raise the blinds
on evening light so thick, so deliciously rich

it melts our bodies. You hesitate, unwind
your scarf. I know—waiters shrug behind my back,
roll their eyes—they think I'm crazy. But this kind

of light feeds us. What does a small camp
in the woods, a crackling fire, mean to you?
Step out of the trees, take off your damp

coat. Sit by this copper light. You are beautiful
tonight, your lined face bright. This is my gift to you.

SORBET

Hips
swing, turn
spin me through.

HOW A WOMAN COMPETES

Playboy invited twenty-four men, and me, to
New York to cook, to compete, to show our skill.
Those other chefs: all classically trained, all knew
how to impress: ice carvings, salmon, thrilling

dishes. In my hands: a box of salad greens
I'd brought from home. I tenderly washed each leaf
all eyes on me. Then, a quiet filled the room.
That first, crisp bite? The sound of revolution.

HOW TO PLANT EDEN

— for Bill Clinton, after his visit to Chez Panisse

I want to tempt your tongue.
I want to feed you one perfect peach. Just reach
for it. Come to Chez Panisse, come

sit at my table. I could beat all day on the drum
of words: *organic, sustainable, fresh,* but no speech
will truly tempt your tongue.

I want to give you Frog Hollow Farm, the hum
of bees, of heat, of a farmer who knows how to eat
all of it. Come to Chez Panisse, come

pick up your spoon. An hour ago, this peach hung
in sunlight. Take a bite. Do you see why we need
a White House Garden to tempt this country's tongue?

Taste is deeper than speech, deeper than some
working group, some committee in a room, analyzing
it all. Just stop. Come to Chez Panisse, come

bite into one sweet peach. Last time you shrugged
me off. Chose blackberry ice cream.
This time, be tempted. Just you, just your tongue.
Come to Chez Panisse and eat with me. Just come.

HOW TO TAKE CARE
OF YOURSELF

To build a luscious meal embrace the slow.
Begin with just a fork and your own breath.
First seer a cut of steak, then just below
you'll find a crispy fond. Next add sweetbreads.

When brown, deglaze your pan again and pour
it over. See? A double consommé.
Too often we are willing to ignore
these underlayers, to forget deep taste.

A hearty stock will take you hours to build.
You calm your hands, your palms, on pan and spoon.
Now breathe in deep and this rich steam will still
your mind. Now see? You have all afternoon.

So when you're ready, add a splash of cream
and stir. All tending starts, this slow. This deep.

SORBET

Arch
holding strong
my foot's cathedral.

HOW TO FIND
YOUR PRIEST
— for Lulu

I sit at your scrubbed wooden table, in perfect hunger.
You pick up mortar and pestle, a few small olives, garlic.
Outside, grow the flavors of Provence: smoky, sweet.
Like this, you show me, grinding the pestle. *Now, you try it.*

Before you pick up mortar and pestle, olives and garlic,
you say: *it's humble, this small toast.*
Like this, you show me, grinding the pestle. *You try it.*
Garlic, olives, oil. That's it. Don't get fancy, don't show off—

it's humble, this small toast.
I taste and I fall in love: with garlic, with Lulu, with my body.
Garlic, olives, oil. Maybe capers. Don't get fancy,
just taste and breathe. Just try to see.

I taste and I fall in love. Garlic, Lulu, my own body.
Eyes closed, I see the kitchen in Berkeley. My table.
I just taste, and breathe, and then I begin to see
the secret is foraging. To find the farmer who loves olives.

Eyes closed, I see my kitchen in Berkeley. At my table
a farmer tells me about a woman in the hills growing olives.
The secret? Forage for the farmer who loves good olives.
I stand in the market, and she hands me one. I bite its dark skin.

fig | 21

This woman is farming olives out in the hills.
What dish can I build? I think of a hungry man, coming in tonight,
as I stand in the market. The farmer hands me an olive. I bite
and already I feel the weight of the pestle in my hand.

What dish can I build? I think of that hungry man coming in,
and how we will touch each other: farm to table to tongue.
I can feel, already, the weight of the pestle in my hand.
I open my eyes to you, Lulu, oil on your hands. Anointed.

Look: we all touch each other: soil to plate to belly.
Outside grow the flavors of Berkeley: smoky, sweet.
Eyes open, here I am. Oil on my hands. Anointed
I sit at my scrubbed wooden table. In perfect hunger.

HOW TO RAISE
A VICTORY
— for Michelle Obama and her White House Garden

Thank you for sugar snap peas.
> For onions, shallots,
>> dill cilantro parsley chives sorrel sage.

Thank you for a thousand square feet
> for the smell of turned over soil
>> for hungry worms, for growing-fat robins.

Thank you for twenty-five fifth graders
> who went home one night and said
>> *I need clothes I can get muddy.*

Thank you for being willing to fail
> in front of a nation of gardeners,
>> and for telling us about the times you did.

Thank you for bats,
> for wing beats in the night, for making
>> the air fly.

Thank you for the afternoon hour your chef
> doesn't step foot in her car. Instead
>> picks raspberries, for your dinner.

Thank you for building
> what Abigail and Edith and Eleanor and Hillary
> all tried to do.

Thank you for reaching back
> into our collective memory: victory gardens
> of tomatoes, peas, peppers. Healthy, even in war.

Thank you for the crunch
> and burst between our teeth
> that first bite of sweet corn.

Thank you for reminding us
> we are fighting.
> Thank you for showing us how to win.

HOW TO LET YOUR CHILD WALK OUT INTO THE WORLD

— for Fanny

I love best
my mortar and pestle.
Heavy in my hand
the good weight
of bowl on butcher block.

I get up early, before my girl.
I hear her
breathing
in the next room, burrowed
in her small bed.

I go out into the garden,
pick luscious
soft greens,
oregano,
a few tiny tomatoes.

I imagine her day:
who will help her
who will harm her
whose shoes she will admire
who will want to swap desserts.

I wash each lettuce leaf,
then stack them,
nestled together.
I slice each firm
tomato in half.

I will not be there.
But here, in soft morning light,
I grind spices,
making the vinaigrette
she loves best.

I love
her small mouth
full of wishes and needs.
The open bowl of her body
that I get to feed.

SORBET

Pelvis
garden for
one treasured seed.

fig | 27

HOW TO BE FED

— after Chez Panisse burns

No grilled white shrimp, no ricotta salad, no chocolate tart.
In the morning, one charred wooden bench out front.
All day long neighbors walk by, touch some small part.
No Catalan cream and roasted almonds, no champagne.

In the morning, one charred wooden bench out front.
How will the busboys pay their rent?
No Catalan cream, no roasted almonds, no champagne.
Inside, the door to the kitchen is gone, the wall is gone.

How will the busboys pay their rent?
I walk through the rooms of wet wood, smashed windows.
The door is gone, an entire wall gone.
I stand alone by the stove. I watch an orange and gold sunset

through the room of wet wood and smashed windows.
What if the cooks could see guests eating? Lifting forks?
If I stood by the stove, I could watch orange-gold sunsets.
What if we built a pizza oven? Let them watch us flip dough?

What if the cooks could see friends eating? Lifting their forks?
Chez Panisse has always been the family sitting down to eat.
What if we could build an oven? Let them watch us grill dough?
But of course, there's no money. That's what everyone tells me.

Chez Panisse has always been the family sitting down to eat
and now in walk friends, talking, planning: a benefit to rebuild.
Of course, there's no money. That's what I tell myself, again.
But look, donations! Wine, lingerie, and a 19th century sword-cane?

In walk more friends, talking, planning. We'll rebuild!
Now look at our olive oil, untouched. Our wine—smoky, but fine.
And donations! Good wine, lingerie. Even a 19th century sword-cane.
One oak chair remains, and I sit, for a moment. Take a sip of wine.

I look at our olive oil, untouched. I taste my wine: smoky, but fine.
Yes, no shrimp tonight. No ricotta salad. No chocolate tart.
But one oak chair remains, and I sit for a moment. I sip my wine
as all evening, neighbors walk by. Touch some small part of me.

fig | 29

HOW TO BEGIN

My favorite recipe:

Pick one
perfectly
ripe fig
in August.
Place it
on a
white plate.
Eat.

No, it's this:

Cut mint
leaves from
the garden.
Boil water.
Pour over.
Wait.
Now
drink.

HOW TO LOOSEN
YOUR SKIN
— for the garlic peelers

Shukran!

       I pick up the bowl of peeled pearls. *Our pleasure*
say the garlic peelers, laughing, sticky. *Our pleasure.*

It's therapeutic to peel garlic. Your hands slow
on a warm night, then grow thick with fragrant pleasure.

These five women, who live within blocks of Chez Panisse,
have come for years to peel, to eat, to learn the art of pleasure.

The pile of peels grows, thin as the skin on Hazel's eyelid
as she winks, tells the story of a night of pleasure.

Hold one clove to your nose: inhale its dark, musky scent.
You know this smell, this deepness, at the center of pleasure.

How do your hands feel? I ask them, hours into the afternoon.
Hot! They shout, then laugh, their faces flushed with pleasure.

I drop one peeled clove into hot oil, listen to it sing and sizzle.
I close my eyes, breathe, feel my throat open in pleasure.

I force myself to stay. There are so many corners of the world
to save. But I linger. I need one this moment of pleasure.

fig | 31

We have eaten here for a years, the women tell a new chef.
We live here, we grow garlic. And honey, we know pleasure.

And how satisfying to watch the birth of one shining body.
How we remember giving birth! Yes pain, but also pleasure.

And now our children, out in the world, eating, building lives.
Have we done enough? Shown them how to live in pleasure?

I dip my fork, lift the soft bulb to my tongue. We built this room
around one clove of desire. Chez Panisse: a temple to pleasure.

Look, Alice! They call, holding up their overflowing bowl.
This too is your work: to unwrap your own body's longing.

                                        Your own petal of pleasure.

SORBET

Thumbnail
cracks open
everything I need.

fig | 33

HOW TO RISE

— for Steve and his Upstairs Bread

Before flour, before starter, before sea
salt, you look out the window. Study the thick leaven
of the clouds: is it humid? Is the air crackling

with electricity? Yes. Then you begin. Crack
open the jar of starter, inhale the sour smell of the sea
at low tide. No yeast here, just the natural leaven

you started years ago from grape vines. If the leavening
works, the inner structure is rich, the crust perfectly cracked.
Even after baking you want to touch its bones: flour, water, sea

salt. We long for this: the sea, the rising, the cracking wide open.

HOW TO BE LOVED

— for you, eating at Chez Panisse, Tuesday Evening

I lift a burning
branch of rosemary,
I cross the small courtyard.

I touch the air,
I deepen the breeze,
I welcome you.

In the sidewalk box: tonight's menu,
your tongue's plan for the evening.

The smell of roasting meat.
One copper light, shining
on a plain white plate.

Sit here. Thick light
opens like a peach,
infuses the room, your palate.

My waiter brings your aperitif.
Don't open your lips, yet.

Drink in its fizz. Now touch
the bread, tips of fingers to hard crust.
Now break it open. Fall air

fig | 35

an afternoon at grandmother's,
apples, warm oven,
sourdough embrace.

Take one olive.
This is your body, your own skin.

Now a salad of warm greens
chicory picked just hours ago,
hand washed in our kitchen.

You see us, here with you,
under white aprons, copper lamps,
drying each piece of lettuce.

This leaf was shade for a beetle just hours ago.
Look: its delicate arch. Farm light folded into green.

Bring the earth into
your throat. The crunch
of a summer breeze.

Your soup a thin broth, stock
cooked all day. While you
were driving shopping talking working

we were shelling a lobster.
Building your soup.

Lift your spoon?
Your ribcage expands.
The sea rushes in, salty harbor air.

Even if you've never
stood on a dock in sunrise,
never listened to the tide lowering.

Taste tiny root vegetables the shape
of your own fingers. Turnips artichoke parsley

bound in sweet butter.
More wine. Lift one tiny carrot
to your teeth.

You don't like carrots—have never liked carrots—
frozen bags, a hurried dinner when you were a child
dishes, homework, parents working hard—

can this be a carrot?
Maybe you don't even know your own name.

Light, like clarified butter
in the heat of summer. Now
lamb with coriander seeds.

You walked, once,
through Redwoods.
The air tasted like grief.

fig | 37

Finally, a soufflé. A lemon moon rising over
a field of grass nobody has built on yet.

> Breathe out.
> Gently rub the lobes of your lips.
> The room darkens. The light goes

> but this time you are ready for it.
> You are not balancing, anymore.
> You are animal, made of leaves, seeds, grasses.

You, turned over, a rich soil.
You, smelling, of rosemary air.

HOW TO BE FULL

A drizzle of rain
falling on Michelle's garden
the smell of deep green.

> Slice some goat cheese: fresh, young, light
> drizzle with Tuscan oil.

I think of Martine
lifting plates, testing their weight,
striped with summer light.

> Lay thick slices on a plate,
> and garnish with wild parsley.

And the man who walked
in our door, offering us
a whole, wild duck.

> Make breadcrumbs out of whole bread:
> *une baguette* toasted lightly.

Lulu, thank you for
spending a whole day teaching
me about freshness.

fig | 39

Pack breadcrumbs into the skin
of cheese: that fresh blend of tastes.

And Hazel! Who comes
each year to skin a thousand
fragrant garlic bulbs.

Bake until its body warms,
softens. Now smell its fragrance.

At Chez Panisse one
man, softened by our food. He
will choose the rich fig.

Be patient. Wait until the
cheese deepens, sweetens, grows rich.

Bob Cannard's farm, deep
in night, no suburbs, roads, just
a little frog song.

Now make a little salad
but leave the center open.

Across the country
my perfect girl sleeps. I still
leave the porch light on.

If you want, slip in garlic.
Perfectly toasted almonds.

A man, in Turkey,
while we slept, slipped a bowl of
goat milk in our tent.

> One bite of these light, tart greens.
> One bite of this warm, goat cheese.

Your tongue will show you
the way to live in the warm
center of your life.

fig | 41

END NOTES & SOURCES

Research and inspiration for these poems came from the following publications and documentaries:

Coming to my Senses by Alice Waters

The Art of Simple Food by Alice Waters

40 Years of Chez Panisse by Alice Waters and Friends

The Chez Panisse Menu Cookbook by Alice Waters

Chez Panisse Café Cookbook by Alice Waters

Chez Panisse Vegetables by Alice Waters

Alice Waters and Chez Panisse by Thomas McNamee

American Grown: The Story of the White House Kitchen Garden by Michelle Obama

At Elizabeth David's Table preface by Ruth Reichl

M.F.K. Fisher, Julia Child, and Alice Waters: Celebrating the Pleasures of the Table by Joan Reardon

Chowhound: The Perfect Salad: https://www.youtube.com/watch?v=N-h5t1U9RPIU

11 Essential Spices for Indian Cooking: https://www.thekitchn.com/11-essential-spices-for-indian-cooking-223152

Housemade: Legend of the Chez Panisse Fruit Bowl Explained: https://www.sfgate.com/restaurants/article/Legend-of-the-Chez-Panisse-fruit-bowl-explained-13484192.php

Fig Research: https://www.keapbk.com/blogs/keap/romancing-the-fig-what-one-fruit-can-tell-us-about-love-life-and-human-civilization

Chez Panisse recipe for roasted figs: http://www.borrowedsalt.com/blog/2015/8/23/chez-panisse-roasted-figs

QUOTES

Epigraph Quote from *Note to Self: Chef Alice Waters Shares Advice to her Younger Self:* https://www.youtube.com/watch?v=8i3p7y5zhb0

The found poem "How to Begin" and "How to Plant Eden" both use language from Alice Water's memoir *Coming to my Senses*

Back cover quote from the Time series *Firsts: Women Who are Changing the World:* https://time.com/collection/firsts/4898540/alice-waters-firsts/

ACKNOWLEDGMENTS

My thanks to the following publications in which these poems first appeared, sometimes in different form.

"Amuse Bouche" ("Gathering Sweetness") – *Cirque*
"How to Rise" ("Upstairs Bread") – *Architrave*
"How to Change a Thousand Minds" ("The Taste of Light") – *Innisfree*
"How to Find Your Priest" ("Amuse-Bouche for Lulu") - *Modern Poetry Quarterly Review*
"How to Let your Child Walk Out into the World" ("Fanny's Salad") – *Poem*
"How to be Fed" ("Fire") – *The Midwest Quarterly*
"How to Eat the Wild" ("Eating the Wild") – *Edible Alaska*

Thanks to Dr. James Engelhardt who read early versions of these poems. Merci beaucoup to Virginie Duverger for her help with the French phrasing.

A warm thank you to the amazing women at Minerva Rising Press: to my editor Sonya Lara who made these poems stronger, to Abby Lewis and Brooke Schultz for building this book, and especially to Kim, for lifting up the voices of women all across this country.

About the Author

Emily Wall is a poet and Professor of English at the University of Alaska. She holds an M.F.A. in poetry from the University of Arizona. Her poems have been published in journals across the US and Canada and she has been nominated for multiple Pushcart Prizes. Her chapbook *Flame* won the Minerva Rising Dare to Be chapbook prize. She has won a Rasmuson Individual Artist Award as well as two Juneau Arts Council grants. She has five books of poetry: *Fist* and *Flame* are chapbooks published by Minerva Rising Press. *Liveaboard* and *Freshly Rooted* have found homes in Salmon Poetry. Her most recent book *Breaking Into Air: Birth Poems* is published by Red Hen Press. Emily lives and writes in Douglas, Alaska, where she is also the coordinator of the Douglas Food Pantry, serving the hungry of Douglas Island. She can be found online at www.emily-wall.com.

9 781950 811199